An Insight into the Horrors of Partition, Colonialism and Women's Issues:
"A Saga of Oppression, Exploitation and Conflict"

Ishfaq Hussain Bhat

AND I DEDICATE THIS WORK OF MINE

TO MY MENTOR

MR. SHEIJATH SHAFI HUSSAIN LONE

WITHOUT WHOSE RESOLUTE ENCOURAGEMENT,

IT WOULD HAVE BEEN VERY DIFFICULT TO FINISH THE BOOK.

Precis

The book, *An Insight into the Horrors of Partition, Colonialism and Women's Issues: A Saga of Oppression, Exploitation and Conflict,* as the title suggests, explores various forms of oppression – the oppression of men against women in a patriarchal society; the unjust oppression of the colonial forces on the downtrodden natives of the weaker nation; the oppression of women in the course of Partition of India. The book brings to light and thus documents the conflict between the forces of colonialism and the forces of the colonized; and the conflict between the forces of patriarchy and the forces of matriarchy. The book has been divided into three chapters for the convenience of the readers. The first chapter of the book highlights and condemns the oppression, exploitation and presentation/ portrayal of women as the objects of desire and pity in a patriarchal society. The chapter brings to light the fact that women, from the very outset, have been greatly wronged and exploited. They have been deprived of their basic rights and have not been treated as human beings but merely as objects of desire The chapter also talks about various movements which aimed to revolt against these absurd discriminations and thereby tried to uplift the downtrodden women. Thus the chapter aims to debunk and criticize the absurd and unjust distinctions prevalent in the patriarchal society. The second chapter of the book highlights the conflict between the colonizer and the colonized. It highlights and condemns the fact that the colonizers exploited the colonized economically, politically and socially in the name of colonialism as a civilizing mission. The chapter thus condemns the fact that the colonizers presented/ disguised the entire process of colonization as a civilizing mission. The chapter also throws immense light on the efforts of the colonized to redefine and reinterpret their identity that had greatly been distorted by the colonizers who represented the colonized as barbaric, uncivilized and immature. Thus the chapter offers a contrapuntal reading of the entire process of colonization and thereby subverts the basic assumption of the process of colonialism as a civilizing mission. Chapter III of the book is about the horrors of Partition – how it resulted in mass trauma and exodus. Many women and children were abducted. Women were raped, tattooed and then mercilessly butchered. Though the chapter talks about the mass trauma and exodus, it primarily focuses on the miseries of women during the Partition of India. It explores the exploitation of women who neither were safe in the rival communities nor in their own communities and families. They were repeatedly violated by the members of the rival communities and as a result, their own family members killed them because they thought that it was better to kill them rather than expose them to the lust of the men of other communities. Thus it, in a way, emphasizes that women were greatly wronged during the Partition violence.

CONTENTS

Acknowledgements

The author feels great pleasure in acknowledging his debt to his mentor Mr. Shejath Shafi Hussain Lone, who has been very helpful and instrumental in the preparation and creation of this work and thereby, in making the dream come true.

Now Dreams

Are not available

To the dreamers,

Nor songs

To the singers.

In some lands

Dark night

And cold steel

Prevail

But the dream

Will come back,

And the song

Break

Its jail.

_ Langston Hughes

Introduction

The book, *An Insight into the Horrors of Partition, Colonialism and Women's Issues,* aims to explore, highlight and condemn various forms of oppression like the oppression of the downtrodden women in the patriarchal society, colonialism and mass trauma and exodus during the Partition of India. For the convenience of the readers, the book has been organized in three Chapters. Chapter I, "The Problem That Has No Name", attempts to explore the issue of patriarchy vis-à-vis women's oppression by the dominant male members of the society. An attempt has been made to allude to different scholars/philosophers/writers in order to establish the fact that women from the very outset have been greatly wronged, oppressed and marginalized. However, the problem is not left unanswered/unsolved. An attempt is made to provide a counterview by citing many authors/philosophers and by bringing to light the fact that though there have been forces at work to suppress/oppress the downtrodden women, there have also been forces to revolt against this unjust and absurd oppression. Various movements, like Feminist Movement, that strived to empower and uplift women, have also been mentioned and discussed at length. And this is followed by the conclusion which the reader shall come to know himself after having read the chapter. Chapter II of the book titled "Post-colonialism: A Conflict Between the Orient and the Occident," is about colonialism: how the Europeans/British presented the entire process of colonization as a civilizing mission and how the natives were exploited and oppressed socially, politically and economically; how attempts were also made to instill a deep repugnance in the minds of the downtrodden natives for their own culture. The chapter aims to bring to light a conflict between the Orient and the Occident. The chapter also highlights the postcolonial posture/strain of different authors who tried to "write back" in order to reinvent, rediscover and restore their lost identity that had greatly been distorted by the colonizers, who portrayed the colonized as barbaric, sinister, undeveloped, immature and uncivilized. Thus the chapter presents a critique of the entire process of Colonization. Chapter III, "Partition of India: A Tale of Mass Trauma, Exodus and Women's Exploitation," is about the partition of India. The chapter aims to provide a deep insight into various hardships that the downtrodden people faced during the communal violence in the course of the partition. However, special attention has been paid to explore, highlight and condemn the miseries and sufferings of women, who, in the course of Partition violence had greatly been wronged. They had not only been wronged by the members of the rival community but also by their own family/community members. The chapter thus brings to light the fact that, during the Partition of India, 'honour killings' and 'gendered violence' became commonplace: Women were not only abducted, tattooed and killed by the members of other communities but their own family members killed them because they thought that it was better to kill them rather than expose them to the members of other communities.

CHAPTER I

THE PROBLEM THAT HAS NO NAME

"I am a slave, a favoured slave

At best to share his pleasure and seem very blest,

When weary of these fleeting charms and me,

There yawns the sack and yonder rolls the sea,

What! Am I then a toy for dotards play

To wear but till the gilding frets away."

From the title page of Child's The History of the Condition of Women.

Introduction:

"Woman is not the useless repetition of man but the enchanted space where the living alliance of man and nature occurs. If she disappeared men would be alone, foreigners without passports in a glacial world. She is earth itself carried to life's summit, the earth becomes sensitive and joyful; without her, for men, earth is mute and dead."

Michel Carrouges

Prejudice based on gender has always been deeply rooted in all cultures. The degree may differ, but the bias and prejudice has always been there. The discourse about women and their miseries occupies a seminal position in the world literature. Women as inferior 'Other' have always been marginalized by the so-called superior 'Man'. They have been deprived of even their basic rights. The patriarchal bias and prejudice of the male-dominated society in general and the anti-feminist philosophers, authors and educators in particular, becomes evident from their portrayal of women as mere objects of desire and pity. From the very outset, they have greatly been wronged. They have been, in a way, forcibly enslaved by inculcating in them a sense of inferiority, weakness, submissiveness, passiveness, servility, and the like. Right from the outset, they have been taught to be submissive, subservient, coquettish, shy which represent ideal womanhood and feminine sensibility. Women have been greatly wronged by the male and biased members of the society. Women as the marginalized 'Other' have been denied freedom of choice, thought and decision making. Men have always been portrayed as beings of reason; and on the contrary, women are presented as mere creatures of affection who do not have an identity of their own. Betty Friedan subtly and artistically questions this distorted representation of women by patriarchy in her seminal work *The Feminist Mystique :* "For the women, in all the columns, books and articles by the experts telling women their role was to seek fulfillment as wives and mothers...Experts told them how to catch a man and keep him, how to breastfeed children and handle their toilet training...how to buy a dishwasher, bake bread, cook...how to dress, look, and act more feminine and make marriage exciting...They learned that truly feminine women do not want careers, higher education, political rights – the independence...A thousand expert voices applauded their femininity, their adjustment, their new maturity. All they had to do was to devote their lives from earliest girlhood to finding a husband and bearing children... They had no thought for the unfeminine problems of the world outside the home, they wanted the men to make the major decisions. They glorified in their role as women, and wrote proudly on the census blank 'Occupation: Housewife'." This chapter showcases women's status/position vis-à-vis men by alluding to different authors; the movements, theories and approaches that have been developed to empower women have also been dealt with in detail. And this would be followed by presenting the contemporary picture/status of the issue, and conclusion.

Views of Different Scholars about Women

Women as the 'Other' have almost always been portrayed as insignificant objects of pity. Most of the scholars upheld the subjugation of women and tried their level best to imprison women in the chains of domesticity. Scholars like Aristotle, Plato, Rousseau, Dr. Gregory, to name a few, believed and advocated that women have been created to serve and please their dominant, superior counterparts, the 'Man'. They viewed women as subservient and inferior to men.

Plato's Views

Plato, a notable Greek philosopher, viewed women to be inferior to men. He believed that women are weaker than men. He assigned to them the traditional roles in the home especially catering to every need of the superior race i.e. men. In his famous work *Republic*, Plato, about the relationship between men and women, states:

"Women and men have the same nature in respect to the guardianship of the state, same insofar as the one is weaker and the other is stronger."

Aristotle's Views on Subjugation of Women

Aristotle, the most famous disciple of Plato, held similar views about women's relationship with men. He too, like his predecessor, viewed women to be inferior to men. He even went ahead and equaled women with slaves of men- the embodiment of the intellectual faculty: "The relation of male to female is by nature a relation of superior to inferior and ruler to ruled." (Aristotle, Politics). He goes on to say, "The male is by nature more expert at leading than female, and the elder and complete than the younger and incomplete... The slave is wholly lacking the deliberative element; the female has it but it lacks authority; the child has it but it is incomplete." (Aristotle, Politics)

In Book IX of his work *History of Animals*, Aristotle talks about the binarism – he associates weakness, falsehood, and the like qualities with women; and the opposite qualities like strength, bravery with men: "Women are more compassionate and more readily made to weep... she is also more shameless and false... more idle... On the contrary, the male is more ready to help... braver than the female."

Rousseau and His Theory of Education for Women

Jean-Jacques Rousseau, the eighteenth-century, believed in the moral superiority of the patriarchal family. He claims that women are subversive to unity and order of the polity. He denied women citizenship rights and he demanded that women be educated differently: they should be educated in order to be able to serve the morally superior being/man properly. Rousseau, who championed French Revolution was not in favour of equality of the sexes. He views about the relation of man and woman gets exemplified when he states: "All the education of women should be relative to men...Woman is made to yield to man and to bear his injustices." Rousseau, like many other writers, propounded that women should be educated in such a way so that they, in a way, learn and inculcate the notions of ideal womanhood and feminine sensibility whereby they would act as delicate and pleasing objects of desire. Rousseau's belief in the moral superiority of the patriarchal family gets manifested in his work *Emile*. Sophie, the heroine in his work *Emile*, is presented as a representative of ideal womanhood who is educated to be governed by her husband, Emile; and on the contrary, Emile, as a representative of the ideal man is educated to govern his family. Rousseau, thus, advocates the subjugation of women for he considers women to be inferior to men.

John Gregory and His *A Father's Legacy to His Daughters*

John Gregory, the eighteenth-century Scottish physician, medical writer and moralist holds similar views about women. Dr. Gregory's *A Father's Legacy to His Daughters* can be used as a manifesto of the patriarchal society which associates qualities like weakness, passiveness, submissiveness, servility and 'emotions' with the feminine. In this work, he advises his daughters on the issues of religion, conduct and behaviour, amusements, friendship and, love and marriage. He wants his daughters to inculcate certain virtues and accomplishments which in turn will render them most honourable and most amiable in the eyes of the 'superior bread' – Man. He tries to instill in them, a deep sense and regard for ideal womanhood and feminine sensibility: "When a girl ceases to blush, she has lost the most powerful charm of beauty. [However] that extreme sensibility which it indicates, may be a weakness and incumbrance in our sex." He also believes that men are superior to women. Moreover, the wit, the intellectual faculty, according to him is the most dangerous talent that they can possess. He even advises then not to display their good sense for it will be thought that they assume a superiority over other rational beings i.e. men – the embodiment of the intellectual faculty. He, in a way, wants his daughters to inculcate all the virtues that the patriarchal society approves and feels fit for the feminine. Moreover, he does not want them to affect delicacy but he wants them to possess it. He advises them to cultivate a fondness for dress and thus, like all other people governed by patriarchal bias, propounds artificiality, affectedness, and the like: "Dress is an important article in female life. The love of dress is natural to you."

Some Textual Evidences and Instances of Women's Subjugation

Most of the writers have presented women as objects of pity and desire who have been created/formed to be subjugated by the rational and superior being/man. Women in order to be quintessentially feminine ought to sacrifice all their independence/freedom. She ought to please man even at the cost of her self-worth and self-identity. Male aristocracy has always precluded women from the decision-making process and thus suppressed their freedom of choice and made them objects of pity.

Henric Ibsen's *A Doll's House*

The treatment and suppression of women gets manifested in Henric Ibsen's play A Doll's House through the character of Nora. Nora states:

"I have been greatly wronged, Torvald – first by papa and then by you... When I was at home with papa, he told me his opinion about everything, and so I had the same opinions; and if I differed from him I concealed the fact, because he would not have liked it. He called me his doll-child, and he played with me just as I used to play with my dolls. And then I came to live with you... I was simply transferred from papa's hand into yours. You arranged everything according to your own taste, and so I got the same tastes as yours... When I look back on it, it seems to me as if I had been living here like as a poor woman – just from hand to mouth... You and papa have committed a great sin against me. It is your fault that I have made nothing of my life... Our home has been nothing but a play room. I have been your doll-wife, just as at home I was papa's doll-child." (Ibsen, 158-160)

Kamala Das's Poem *An Introduction*

Kamala Das artistically portrays the suppression and subjugation of women in a patriarchal society in most of her poems. But, here, we shall focus on her poem An Introduction. In the following lines of the poem, she subtly and elegantly presents the enforced subjugation of women whereby they are asked to "fit in," and "belong":

"Dress in Sarees, be girl,

Be wife, they said. Be embroiderer, be cook,

Be a quarreler with servants. Fit in, oh!

Belong, cried the Categorizer. Don't sit

On walls and peep in through our laced-

drapped Windows.

Be amy, or be Kamala. Or better

Still, be Madhavikutty. It is time to

Choose a name, a role."

A COUNTERVIEW

Feminism: Background/History

The term feminism came into use in English in 1890. Its origins can be traced back to the abolitionist movement of 1830s. However, the contemporary concept of feminist movement began in the 1960s when divorce became commonplace, and when women were beginning to find fulfillment outside the realm of domesticity and, they were no more "happy house-wives"; and when higher level of employment and fulfillment outside the four walls of home were becoming a norm. During enlightenment, the egalitarian, the reformist and the liberal ideas were, to some extent, extended to women. In the 19th century, movements like abolition of slavery, Temperance Movement, and struggle to grant women voting rights played a significant role in the conscious raising of women.

Feminism Defined

Feminism is a movement that aims to revolt against the patriarchal society which associates superiority, action, strength, self-assertion and domination with the 'masculine' and on the contrary, inferiority, passivity, weakness, obedience and self-negation with the 'feminine' or the 'Other'. Feminism advocates women's rights on the ground of equality of sexes by defining and establishing social, legal and cultural freedom and equality of women. Feminists, by depicting the miseries of women in their works, highlight and condemn the plight of women in the patriarchal society and thereby try to inculcate in them a sense of rebellion, self-assertion, self-identity and self-worth. Jessica Valenti aptly defines feminism in the following terms: "Feminism isn't simply being a woman in a position of power. It's battling systematic inequities; it's a social justice movement that believes sexism, racism, and classism exist and interconnect, and that they should be consistently challenged." Feminism advocates the empowerment of women and that it can be achieved by ending the absurd gender inequalities. Women, according to Feminists, are to be given equal opportunities in all spheres of life. It advocates the liberation of women from artificial traditional restraints. It advocates the social, political, and economic equality of the sexes. The hallmark of this movement is to demonstrate the importance of women and to highlight and condemn the fact that historically women have been subordinate to men.

PERIODIZATION OF FEMINIST MOVEMENT

First-Wave Feminism

"It was a period of feminist activity and thought that occurred within the time period of the 19th and early 20th century throughout the world. It focused on legal issues, primarily on gaining women's suffrage." Elizabeth Candy Stanton and Susan B Anthony of USA published *"The Revolution"* which in real sense of the term, brought revolution by educating women about their basic rights and, in a way, ushered in the second-wave of feminism. The Equal Rights Party nominated Victoria Woodhull as the first woman Presidential candidate.

Second-Wave Feminism

This wave of feminism waned between the two world wars and was revived in late 1960s and early 1980s. In this stage of feminism, in addition to political rights, social, economic rights to fight for greater equality in education, at workplace and at home were demanded. It advocated for the removal of gender inequality and oppression. It was during this period that liberal, radical and socialist streams of feminism emerged.

Third-Wave Feminism

It includes the period from the 1990s to the present. It says that there are differences even among the women due to race, ethnicity, class, nationality and religion. Gender struggle is due to the search for identity. This phase is marked by more expansion and transformation of the feminist movement. Feminism now does not only include social, political and legal rights, but it includes empowerment of women. Feminists now ask for parity with the powers which are enjoyed by men.

Objectives of These Movements

All these waves aimed to change the stereotypical image of women as objects of pity. These movements sought to achieve economic independence of women and give them freedom in terms of choice and decision making. These waves criticized the patriarchal notion of women as objects of desire and propounded that they were not mere objects of pity and desire but were more empowered, more sensible and more substantial. Another aim and feature of these movements was to advance women's participation in political decision making and areas of public life since women were precluded in the decision making process every now and then.

Different Approaches and Theories of Feminism

Approaches

Different approaches have been employed to tackle 'the problem that has no name'. The Essentialist Feminist Approach advocates that gender differences are important and they must be fixed. The Liberal Feminist Approach states that men and women are equal, differences in abilities are trivial. It strives for including women working outside traditional gender roles as subjects of study. The Postmodern Feminist Approach advocates that there are differences which are important but these differences are arbitrary and flexible.

Theories

a) Liberal Feminist Theory: It states that all people are created equal and should not be denied equality of opportunity because of gender. It focuses on social change through the construction of legislation and regulation of employment practices. Cynthia Enloe's contribution is very important: she states that women are very substantial: they have played central roles in combat – as nurses, journalists, and it is they who provide secure home front. It defines feminine in terms of two claims: normative and descriptive. Normative (what ought to be) says that women are entitled to equal rights and respect. The Descriptive (what is the reality) says that women are disadvantaged with respect to rights and respects when compared to their dominant counterparts.

b) Radical Feminist Theory: It blames patriarchal society for all the woes of women. It states that patriarchy has always oppressed women by subjugating them, and that the root cause of all other inequalities is the oppression of women. However, later radicals acknowledge the differences based on gender identity.

c) Cultural Feminist Theory: This theory states that there are fundamental personality differences between men and women. Women's differences make them special and, therefore, it should be celebrated. It advocates the governance of women for women are kinder and gentler then men, and that if women ruled the world there would be no wars. The central strain of this theory is that "woman's way" is the best way.

d) Eco-Feminist Theory: It states that male ownership of land has lead to a domineering culture – it has resulted in the absurd gender discriminations and inequalities. The degeneration of nature because of the patriarchal hold results in the degeneration of women's status. The male domination and exploitation of women is the core of the eco-feminist analysis.

Views of Different Authors Who Championed the Cause of Women

Many writers, especially feminists have tried to 'write back' in order to liberate women from the chains of subjugation, artificiality and domesticity. By virtue of conscious raising awareness, they have, in a way, succeeded in subverting the biased patriarchal notions and absurd gender distinctions prevalent in the patriarchal society. Writers like Mary Wollstonecraft, Betty Friedan, Simone de Beauvoir, to name a few, have championed the cause of women.

Michel de Montaigne's Views

Montaigne while supporting women's cause wrote: "Women are not wrong at all when they reject the rules of life that have been introduced into the world, insomuch as it is the men who have made these without them. There is a natural plotting and scheming between them and us." But he does not go so far as to champion their cause.

Dennis Diderot on the Empowerment of Women

Diderot, the 17th century feminist, claims that though there is a difference between the anatomy of men and women, but it does not reveal a privilege for the male. Moreover, he upholds a solid education for women.

Poullain de La Barre's Views

Poulain de la Barre, a little-known 17th century feminist, was critical of the writings of the male/patriarchal society. His criticism of the portrayal of women by the writers governed by the patriarchal bias becomes evident from his statement: "Everything that men have written about women should be viewed with suspicion, because they are both judge and party."

Montesquieu

Montesquieu, the 18th century French lawyer, wonders that why women, who govern the home, are not allowed to reign outside the realm of domesticity. He states: "It is against reason and against nature for women to be mistresses in house…but not for them to govern an empire."

John Stuart Mill

John Stuart Mill, the 19th century British philosopher, was the only mainstream philosopher to espouse the cause of women and enfranchise them. Debunking the traditional notion of women to be subordinate to men, he states: "The principle which regulates the existing social relations between the two sexes – the legal subordination of one sex to the other – is wrong in itself…it ought to be replaced by a principle of perfect equality."

Mary Wollstonecraft

Mary Wollstonecraft, with the publication of her *A Vindication of the Rights of Women* in 1792, brought a revolution as far as the upliftment of the downtrodden women is concerned. Mary, who became the protagonist of the feminist movement, had gone through crisis of the family: how her mother and her sister were tortured, how her sister got abused in a marriage; all these experiences lead to develop her notion of feminism. In her landmark work, *A Vindication of the Rights of Women*, Mary highlights and condemns the false system of education and absurd notions of patriarchy found in the books written by the so-called rational and intellectual creatures. She also criticizes the tendency of the male writers of rendering females merely as women rather than human beings. Mary Wollstonecraft championed the cause of women. She advocated their independence from the absurd and artificial restrictions and chains of domesticity. In her seminal work, she highlights and condemns Rousseau's treatment of women who propounds that women should be educated differently. He proposed this type of education for women in the chapter entitled 'Sophy, or the Woman' in Book V of his famous work *Emile*. Mary directly criticises Rousseaue in her book: "Rousseau declares that women should never for a moment feel independent, that she should be governed by fear to exercise her natural cunning, and made a coquettish slave in order to render her a more alluring object of desire, a sweeter companion to man…whenever he chooses to relax himself…because with respect to the female character, obedience is the grand lesson which ought to be impressed with unrelenting rigour."

Efforts of Susan B Anthony and Elizabeth Candy Stanton

Susan and Stanton played a deterministic role for the upliftment of American women. They strived for giving women right to vote and were the leading figures of the suffrage movement. For the empowerment of women, they set up Women's Loyal National League in 1863, which was the first national women's political organization in the United States. In 1968, they began publishing a weekly newspaper called "*The Revolution*" for the cause of women. Although it only lasted for a few years, it was successful enough to spread their opinions and was equally instrumental to keep up their campaign for women to be allowed to vote.

Present Scenario

Women, it must be acknowledged, have been greatly empowered vis-à-vis their wretched position in the past. Many organizations have been established from time to time for the cause of women. Many measures have been taken all over the world to strengthen the position of women vis-à-vis men. If we talk of our country, India, there has occurred a drastic change in the status of women: Woman, who had no self-worth in the traditional patriarchal society and would bury herself alive on the funeral pyre of her husband, has now become enlightened and empowered enough to be the head of the state. The schemes like Beti Bachao Beti Padhao have played a deterministic role in the upliftment of women. The Beti Bachao Beti Padhao scheme was launched in 2015 to address the issue of the declining child sex ratio. Sex selective abortion has lead to this decline. It is believed that dowry system prevalent in India is a major cause for female foeticide. Women who have always been considered inferior to men are supposed to give a large dowry to get married to the rationally, intellectually, morally and physically superior being in the patriarchal society. Though Olympic 2016 Bronze medalist, Sakshi Malik, was made brand ambassador of Beti Bachao Beti Padhao, the miseries of women have not ended. Though many measures have been taken all over the world to strengthen the position of women vis-à-vis the 'superior' being, even in the 21st century, they are still treated as dolls. They are still denied the freedom of choice, freedom to stand on their own feet, freedom to live a life of dignity, and freedom to take decisions on their own. The deeply entrenched prejudice and bias of the patriarchal society, whereby the freedom and the decision making powers of a woman are curtailed, is best exemplified in the 'Hadiya Love Jihad Case'. The case of Hadiya, a Hindu girl, who married a Muslim boy last December, shows how, even in the present enlightened period, women are not given their due. The courts have treated her as someone without the right to choose how to live, whom to marry, or even to assert that she has a husband who can support her. It is quite evident that if it was a man in Hadiya's place, the court would have responded differently. If it was a man in

Hadiya's place, he would not have been in court and people would not have objected to his marriage either. The annulment of Hadiya's marriage without her consent, in a way, questions the partiality of the patriarchal society in general and judiciary in particular. Though she is an adult, she was placed under the guardianship of her father. If it was a man in her place, the court would have certainly responded differently. Cases like Hadiya's highlight the fact that even in the 21st century women, despite having many powers, are still denied freedom to choose how to live their own life, whom to love, what creed to follow, how to keep body and soul together. And it certainly raises the question; whether women are considered human beings at all?

Conclusion:

To wrap up the discussion, many things need to be brought together. Scholars, philosophers and writers have opined different opinions on the topic of women's position vis-à-vis men. Scholars like Plato, Aristotle, Rousseau, to name a few have greatly marginalized and sidelined women. They propounded that the relationship between man and woman is that of a superior and inferior, or master and slave. On the contrary, many scholars, especially feminists, condemn the forced enslavement of the feminine and advocate freedom of women from the clutches/chains of domesticity. There have been extremist views on both the sides: One group overtly believes that man is the master and woman a slave, and that, woman have naturally been created/formed to be an 'inferior being' that has to cater to every need of the 'Superior Other'. The other group, in contrast, does not only want parity with the powers enjoyed by men but it, in a way, wants/tries to overpower the other group. However both the views are extreme. The need of the hour is to find a way out in between these two extremist views. The opinion of Recep Tayyib Erdogan seems to be the best way to address/settle the issue. Erdogan rightly states, "What women need is to be able to be equivalent, rather than equal, because equality turns the victim into an oppressor and vice versa." Erdogan goes on to say that though women have overshadowed men in many aspects of life, there are certain fields/jobs that do not suit women: "You cannot make women work in the same jobs as men do, as in communist regime. You cannot give them a shovel and tell them to do their work. This is against their delicate nature." Though this opinion may, apparently, seem patriarchal, but it is essential to elevate or rather protect the dignity of the being that is different in many ways from the man. However, this should not mean that women should once again be plunged into the sea of subjugation; they should be given their due and that their self-identity and self-worth should never be distorted and challenged. It is an established fact that women have greatly been wronged by men by considering women mere objects of desire and depriving them of their basic rights. They have almost always been ill-treated. The main reason behind the lack of progress is that women have been deprived of playing the role they have been created for. However, women through their unrelenting efforts, and with the efforts of different organizations and government schemes, are trying to define their self-worth and self-identity. No doubt their participation outside the realm of the four walls of the house, characterized by their presence and participation at the highest decision making bodies is improving, but we still have not been able to give them their due. The patriarchal notions are still deeply entrenched in the modern society which considers women to be inferior and employs different methods to subjugate the 'feminine'. There are still many Hadiyas in the world who do not have a freedom of choice and decision making. It is high time that we, in a way, transform/replace Hadiya with Daisy of R. K. Narayan's novel *The Painter of Signs*: when she was asked to parade before a prospective bridegroom, she replied that she was not going to be inspected by anyone instead she would inspect the groom. Betty Friedan rightly and subtly states: "The problem that has no name stirring in the minds of so many women today is not a matter of loss of femininity or too much education, or the demands of domesticity. It is far more important than anyone recognizes. It is the key to these other new problems which have been torturing women and their husbands and children... for years... We can no longer ignore that voice within women that says: "I want something more than my husband and my children and my home." The need of the hour is to inculcate a feeling of togetherness among the two sexes and to educate men about women's issues. There is an immense need to empower women by providing them equal opportunities in all spheres of life like education, health, nutrition, politics and above all, decision making. However, this does not mean that women should be so empowered that the life of the men becomes miserable. It would not be wrong to end the chapter with a quotation from Jawaharlal Nehru; "To awaken the people, it is the women who must be awakened. Once she is on the move, the family moves, the village moves, the nation moves."

References and Further Readings

Friedan, Betty. *The Feminine Mystique*. W. W. Norton and Co. 1963.

Wollstonecraft, Mary. *A Vindication of the Rights of Women*. 1792.

Gregory, John. *A Father's Legacy To His Daughters.*

Rousseau, Jean-Jaques. *Emile, Or On Education*. 1762.

Woolf, Virginia. *A Room of One's Own*. 1929.

Ibsen, Henric. A Doll's House. 1879.

Narayan, R. K. The Painter of Signs.1976.

Adichie, Chimamanda Ngogi. We Should All Be Feminist.2014.

Beauvoir, Simone de. The Second Sex. Translated by Constance Borde and Sheila Malovancy-Chevallier; with an introduction by Judith Thurman.

Barre, Francois, Poullain de la. The Equality of the Two Sexes.1673

Anthony, Susan B; Stanton, Elizabeth Candy. The Revolution. 1868-72.

Balzac, Honore de. *Letters of Two Brides*; translated by R. S. Scott.

Child, Lydia, Maria. The History of the Condition of Women,

in Various Ages and Nations

CHAPTER II

Post-colonialism: A Conflict between the Orient and the Occident.

"East is East, and West is West

And never the twain shall meet."

_Rudyard Kipling

Introduction

Post-colonialism relates to colonialism which was a political phenomenon. Post-colonialism, thus, has clear overtones of politics. During the 18th and 19th centuries some of the European countries occupied the weaker nations of Latin America, Middle East, Africa and Asia. The powerful countries like Britain, France and, Netherlands colonized the weaker nations like India, Congo, Brazil, Egypt, etc and hence the process came to be called as colonization. In this chapter, I will be focusing on the Great Britain because we in India were colonized by the British. This phenomenon of colonialism also affected literature just as it did other aspects of life. Literature would not have remained unaffected by this powerful phenomenon. Michel Foucault has rightly and aptly said: "Knowledge and power are closely related and it is power which determines the course of knowledge." So the imperial power, the British in India, would obviously have their own kind of system of education so that the Indians can be subjugated and subjected to their rule, dominance and superiority so much that these two hundred years were so long that Indian conscious and subconscious mind is still preoccupied with inferiority vis-à-vis the superior and civilized

British. In most Indians, it is engraved that the British are the superior people. This precisely is what they wanted. They hammered it in our minds that they are civilizing us by giving us education, by establishing schools and colleges. by giving new knowledge of science and technology and, above all, by giving the language and culture embedded in the English language. This was their colonial mission/programme.

Ramifications of Colonialism.

After the British left India in 1947, by that time they had left most of the countries. The phenomenon of decolonization actually began right after World War I came to an end in 1918. And after that it continued until the end of the World War II in 1945. So, by 1950s most countries were liberated from the enforced slavery/colonization. So this phenomenon of colonization and decolonization obviously had its own repercussions in the education, culture, literature, arts, and every aspect of life of the colonized nations. Therefore, the literature produced during that period was heavily influenced by the ideas of the Enlightenment of the colonizer. These lights of enlightenment were, in a way, thrust upon the colonized and that they, the downtrodden, were made to feel as if a massive favour was being done to them: that the colonized were transformed from the primitive, barbarian, uncivilized society to a modern, enlightened, and civilized society/nation. This resulted in the suppression of a thousand years old civilization of the colonized. The colonized were made to believe that their civilization was just primitivism, absence of culture and civilization and, therefore, they must now learn the more enlightened, civilized and rich traditions of the colonized. This in turn resulted in the cultural and, in a way, psychological colonization of the weaker nations.

Post-colonialism

"Postcolonial as we define it does not mean post-independence or 'after colonialism' for this would falsely ascribe an end to the colonial process. Post-colonialism, rather, begins from the very first moment of the colonial contact. It is the discourse of oppositionality which colonization brings into being." (Ashcroft, Griffiths, Tiffin, 117). Post-colonialism is an academic discipline that analyses, explains and responds to the cultural legacy of colonialism and imperialism. Post-colonialism speaks about the human consequences cultural control and economic exploitation of the native people and its lands. Drawing from Postmodernism school of thought, Post-colonialism studies analyze the politics of knowledge, control and distribution. As a genre of the contemporary history, Post-colonialism questions and reinvents the manner in which the culture is being viewed, challenging the narratives espousing in the colonial era and psychologically, it records relations between the colonialist and the people under colonial rule. As a critical theory it explains, and illustrates the ideology and practices of the Colonization with examples drawn from history. It examines the effect of the colonial rule on the cultural aspects of the colony and its treatment of women, language, literature and humanity. Post-colonialism addresses the problem of knowledge, culture, matters that constitute the postcolonial identity of a developing nation: how the western knowledge was applied to subjugate the non-European people into colony of the European mother country, which after the initial invasion was affected by means of the cultural identities of the colonizer and the colonized. In Postcolonial Literature, the anti-conquest narrative analyzes that there are the social, and cultural perspectives of the subaltern colonial subjects. Generally speaking, when we speak of postcolonial literature and Postcolonial criticism, we mean literatures written after the decolonization. But things do not happen so precisely. It actually includes the narratives written before the decolonization even by the colonizers themselves. The term postcolonial text means anti-colonial and it emphasizes the local life and culture of the colonized. This had started right in the realm of the British rule itself as there were writers who had started writing texts which gave a true picture of what India was like and how distortions had come about in the life, culture and literature of the colonized because of the foreign imposition/rule/domination.

Edward Said and 'Orientalism'

Edward Said and his work Orientalism (1978) are associated with the foundation of the postcolonial studies as an academic discipline. The term Orientalism is derived from the root word orient, which refers to the East or things related to the East. Orientalism, according to Said means the "discourse about the orient associated with the military and economic domination of the Orient by Europe." Edward Said's main argument is that European colonial domination of the Orient was integrally associated with how the Orient was conceptualized, researched and talked about in Europe. The military and economic domination of the Orient was tied up with the discourse about the Orient and it is this discourse about the Orient that Said refers to as Orientalism. This builds upon Foucault's argument that power, knowledge and discursive manifestation of knowledge are integrally related with each other. The Orient and the Occident refer to a conceptual binary. Orientalism, in a way, justifies colonization. Orientalism calls Arabs and Indians as savage, barbaric, primitive, sinister, undeveloped and uncivilized and, on the contrary, it presents European colonization as a civilizing mission rather than an exploitative enterprise. The argument that a colonial discourse makes is that colonialism, by exposing these less civilized people to the more civilized Europeans, actually, benefits them more because they get enlightened. It portrays the colonized as barbaric, uncivilized, immature and childlike, who need guidance of the enlightened Europeans. Thus it twists, though in a bizarre way, the colonial reality. According to Said, there are three aspects of Orientalism:

A) Orientalism is a particular way of thinking – build upon contrasting the Orient from the Occident.

B) Orientalism is an academic discipline

C) Orientalism is a corporate institution of dealing with the Orient.

Self-assumed Superiority of the Occident.

The military and economic colonialism is integrally associated with a particular kind of discourse that we call Colonial discourse. The colonizers strived to construct the image or identity of the colonized people and their lands as the "Other". They portrayed them as uncivilized, primitive, barbarized, underdeveloped and immature. On the contrary, they presented the European colonizers as civilized, advanced, mature, and the like. The postcolonial discourse tries to debunk this biased stereotypical image of the natives as barbaric, sinister and immature. Most of the European scholars have not only neglected the miseries and exploitation of the colonized by the European colonizers, but they have even distorted the reality of colonialism by presenting colonization as a civilizing mission. Karl Marx, in spite of being aware of the havoc that British colonialism wrecked in India by destroying its traditional economic and social structures, justified the British rule in India in his article *"The British rule in India"* (1835). Marx's analysis of the colonial situation was marked by a millennia old prejudice that the Orient represents a backward, barbaric, sinister, uncivilized society vis-à-vis the enlightened and civilized European colonizers. Karl Marx states that even though, due to British rule the Indians "lost their ancient forms/customs of civilization, and even hereditary means of sustenance," what was actually lost was, according to Marx, "barbaric customs and ways of living." The British were, according to Marx, ushering in a much needed social revolution. Thus Marx justified the brutal and unjust rule of British as a much needed social revolution because he belonged to the British/colonized. The British who brought about these changes were, ultimately representatives of a superior civilization. Lord Macaulay's prejudice and self-assumed superiority of the Occident is manifested from his following statement: "I have no knowledge of either Sanskrit or Arabic. But...I have conversed both here and at home with men distinguished by their proficiency in the Eastern tongues...I have never found one among them who could deny that a single shelf of a good European library was worth the whole native literature of India and Arabia." (Minutes Upon Indian Education, 2nd February 1835).

"Writing Back": A Counterview

The postcolonial literature began right during the colonial period itself. Post-colonialism, thus, had cropped up in the very face of the colonialism. After the decolonization, we had more bold narratives because now we could more freely and frankly and with guts say things which were not possible to be said during the colonial period. The anti-colonial strain of the writers had started even when the British were here. Tagore, for instance, started writing in the 19th century and he wrote nationalist songs, Geetanjali, etc. However, when he composed them and gave a song like "Jana Gana Mana" he said that supposedly he has written it to welcome George V, the ruler of England, and therefore, the ruler of the English colonies including India; but actually, he was addressing God and not George V. Even before Tagore, writers like Bankim Chandra Chatterjee, wrote strong nationalist piece right in the face of British. So we had this postcolonial strain in literature even in the pre-independence period.

Henry Louis Vivian Derozio: The first Nationalist Poet of Modern India

Henry Louis Vivan Derozio, a 19th century Indian poet, presents a nationalistic posture in most of his poems e.g., "*The Harp of India*," "*My native land*," etc. His famous sonnet artistically portrays the downfall of Indians after their colonization and the hope of future regeneration:

The Harp of India

"Why hang'st thou lonely on yon withered bough?

Unstrung forever, must thou there remain;

Thy music once was sweet – who hears it now?

Why doth the breeze sigh over thee in vain?

Silence hath bound thee with her fatal chain;

Neglected, mute, and desolate art thou,

Like ruined monument on desert plain:

O! many a hand more worthy far than mine

Once thy harmonious chords to sweetness gave,

And many a wreath for them did Fame entwine

Of flowers still blooming on the minstrel's divine

May be by mortal wakened once again,

Harp of my country, let me strike the strain!"

When we read the first eight lines of the poem, we see Derozio is using a broken harp as a metaphoric representation of India. And that he is lamenting about its present state of decay at the hands of the colonizers. The harp whose music was once so sweet has now, due to the foreign domination, fallen into disrepair: "Silence hath bound thee with her fatal chain." (Line 5). The next three and a half lines speak about glory of past. The next two and a half lines introduce a new volta. Here, the poet speaks about the future in which the poet will try to restore the harp by breaking its silence and making it sing again: "Harp of my country, let me strike the strain!" (Line 14). Derozio, here, uses western artistic template to express India's nationalistic thought, which is the hallmark of the postcolonial literature.

Two different patterns employed by Indian Authors as a means of decolonization

There is a cyclic pattern present in Derozio's poetry: glory of a golden past, the degenerated present and, a promise of future recovery back to the glorious golden past. However, in contrast to this cyclic pattern, there was another pattern prevalent in the works of some Indian authors like Bankim Chandra Chatterjee, which advocated a deep regard for the knowledge and cultural values of the colonizer. Though both the patterns were used as a template to script the path towards decolonization and recovery of the golden past, there was a remarkable and basic difference between the two patterns/approaches – while the later had a deep regard for the colonizer's culture and saw colonization as means of civilization; the other pattern, the cyclic pattern, wanted not only decolonization of the land, but had a deep repugnance for the culture of the colonizers. The nationalist writers like Bankim Chandra Chatterjee thought the rule of the British to be essential to teach the currently 'uncivilized and uneducated' people of present India, who had fallen from the glorious past. According to such writers, it was imperative to learn from the Europeans to recover that past glory. Therefore, British with their civilizational virtues were actually seen as good teachers, who could teach the Indians the very same civilizational values which they had once possessed during the golden age but which they have now lost and have fallen into a state of degeneration. However, the later nationalistic leaders and writers like Gandhi, Raja Rao, etc completely rejected this position/posture. Unlike Bankim, they argued that western civilization rather than being a cure, was itself the problem because, the fall of Indian civilization can be traced back to the moment of European colonial subjugation of India.

Gandhi's Argument against "The White Man's Burden"

In his seminal work *Hind Swaraj or Indian Home Rule* (1909), Gandhi subtly states: "The tendency of Indian Civilization is to elevate the moral being; that of the Western Civilization is to propagate immorality. The latter is godless, the former is based on a belief in God." According to Gandhi, the essence of this deeply moral and theistic Indian Civilization had been perfected by the ancestors of the modern day Indians and "it was found true on the anvil of experience." Therefore, for the rich ancestral Indian heritage, there was nothing to learn from anybody else, especially from the supposedly-superior and civilized Europeans. Thus according to Gandhi, any attempt to immolate Indian civilization was for an Indian tantamount to become detached from his or her ancestral heritage and deviating from his or her true identity. According to Gandhi, attempting to imitate westerners is equivalent to 'contracting a disease' – the disease of the 'satanic western civilization.'

Raja Rao's Potcolonial Posture in *Kanthapura*

Raja Rao's novel *Kanthapura* is a representative postcolonial text. As a postcolonial text, *Kanthapura* focuses on the encounter of the two cultures and shows how while countering the imposing culture, the weaker one redefines and reinterprets its tradition while it seeks its identity. Raja Rao subtly and artistically deconstructs the myth of the power of the foreign rule as a civilizing mission and presents the resistance and indianness in the novel as a means to deconstruct this myth. Raja Rao's indianization of the novel form and emphasis on the decolonization of English language can be interpreted from the postcolonial perspective. Raja Rao did not consider English language to be an alien language but he claimed it to be the language of "our own intellectual make-up." By deviating from the conventional and British ways of writing novels, Raja Rao produced literature in an alien language yet native in style. Raja Rao's juxtaposition of Indian freedom struggle with Ramayana, his Puranic art of narration and, his indianization of the novel makes *Kanthapura* a quintessential postcolonial text. In *Kanthapura*, Raja Rao shows a remarkable parallelism between Ramayana and the freedom struggle of India. This in turn gives *Kanthapura* a typical postcolonial posture. He represents swaraj as Sita, Mahatama as Rama and Nehru as Bharatha. He gives a religious posture to the novel when he compares Rama's journey to Lanka to bring Sita, to Gandhi's trip to England to participate in the Second Round Table Conference: "They say the Mahatama will go to the Red-Man's country and he will get us Swaraj. He will bring us swaraj, the Mahatama. And we shall all be happy. And Rama will come back from exile and Sita will be with him, for Ravana will be slain and Sita freed, he will come back with Sita on his right in his chariot of the air and brother Bharatha will go to meet them with the worshipped sandal of the master on his head. And as they enter Ayodhya, there will be a rain of flowers."

Heart of Darkness and The Colonial Discourse

The postcolonial literature does not only include works written by the previously colonized people after the decolonization but also the works written by the colonizers about the colonized. Many British writers have written about the colonization of the non-European nations by the stronger European nations. Joseph Conrad, the British novelist, in his seminal novel *Heart of Darkness* (1889), presents the relation between the British and the people of the

Congo. The title of the novel symbolizes the portrayal of non-Europeans as ignorant, primitive, undeveloped and uncivilized. In the colonial discourse, Africa was frequently referred to as the Dark Continent. This darkness symbolizes lack of knowledge, primitiveness, and ignorance. The Occident thought that the Orient was not enlightened enough to differentiate between what was morally good and what was morally bad. On the contrary, Europe symbolized forces of light, civilization, and knowledge because it was perceived as progressive and mature. Therefore, according to them, it was a divine obligation on them to civilize and enlighten the barbarian people. Conrad presents the Congo as an infamous site of inhuman colonial brutalities and exploitation. *Heart of Darkness* is, in a way, a documentation of these European brutalities meted out on the colonized. In the novel, the character Charles Marlow is commissioned by the Belgian company to take charge of a boat that plied along the Congo River and locate a mysterious person called Kurtz. Marlow takes time to grasp what is happening around him precisely because, as a European fed on the myth of colonialism as a mission of civilizing the barbaric natives, he finds it difficult to make sense of the reality that is so far removed any trace of civilizing the people and of progress. Kurtz is presented as an iconic European – a superior being. He is greatly praised for procuring an astonishing amount of ivory from Africa to be shifted to Europe. The extraction and transportation of ivory, one of the most precious resources of the Congo, from Africa to Europe, represents the economic exploitation of the colonized. This, in turn, turns the justification of colonialism on the part of the Colonizer on its head. This shows that the basis for colonialism was not so much political as economic. Moreover, the exploitation and brutality of the colonizers becomes evident when Marlowe sees Kurtz's house for the first time. When he sees it through his binoculars, he is stunned to see the numbers of poles surrounding the house with dried and shrunken heads of Africans which Kurtz had severed from the bodies of the native villagers to spread terror among the natives. Conrad's description of this callousness on the part of Kurtz symbolizes the forced enslavement of the natives and how they were economically exploited by the colonizers who forced/terrorized them to hunt for ivory. Thus, Conrad's novel turns the colonial discourse on it head and explodes the myth of civilizing mission by placing it against the brutal realities of colonialism. Hence, *Heart of Darkness* manifests, in a way, Conrad's contrapuntal reading of the colonial discourse for it attempts to read the colonial discourse against the ideological bias that underlines it. *Heart of Darkness* brings out the contradiction, prejudice, bias and falsehood that underline the colonial discourse.

E. M. Forster and his *A Passage to India*

E. M. Forster's *A Passage to India* is another novel in the genre of Postcolonial Literature. Forster, who worked in India as a secretary to Maharaja, shared his experience of living in India and his comprehension of India and Indian people in his seminal novel *A Passage to India*. Forster artistically portrays the self-assumed superiority of the British. This is manifested in the episode whereby Aziz is summoned by his boss, Major Callender and when Aziz goes to meet him, Mr Callender has already left the house without leaving a message for him. To add insult to injury, his *tonga* is also carried away by two English women. This episode shows the lifelong prejudice and self-assumed superiority of the British. This biased attitude of the colonizers is also manifested in the Bridge Party episode in the novel. In this party, the British avoid mixing up with the Indians because they consider themselves to be the representatives of the more civilized, superior and enlightened race. Though he highlighted the racial prejudice of the British in the novel, he, being an English colonizer, had his own limitations. He saw it through the coloured glasses of an English ruler of a supposedly superior civilization.

CHENUA ACHEBE AS THE REPRESENTATIVE POSTCOLONIAL WRITER

Despite Conrad's depiction of the miseries of the Africans in the novel, there are certain descriptions which manifest even the bias of Conrad himself. Chinua Achebe's essay "*An image of Africa: Racism in Conrad's Heart of Darkness*" (1988) is a seminal essay for it subverts/debunks the description of the colonized and their lands as barbaric, sinister and uncivilized. The fundamental argument of Achebe in the essay is that the way the image of Africa was constructed by the colonizing Europeans was guided by an important psychological need in them. By portraying Africa and its people as savage, uncivilized, brutish and barbaric, the colonizers were creating a foil for themselves so that they could themselves appear in a positive light. Conrad's criticism of the colonial discourse was a partial criticism because "in spite of his criticism, Conrad shared the most fundamental idea which informed the colonial discourse in Africa: that the Africans were lesser human beings than the Europeans. Conrad's partial and biased description of the Africans can be seen in the following lines:

"And we struggled round a bend, there would be a glimpse of rush walls, of peaked grass-roofs, a burst of yells, a whirl of black limbs, a mass of hands clapping, of feet stamping, of bodies swaying, of eyes rolling, under the droop of heavy and motionless foliage... The prehistoric man was cursing us, praying to us, welcoming us – who could tell?"

It becomes evident from the above lines that Conrad/Marlow categorizes the Africans as "prehistoric men" and this symbolizes that Conrad/Marlow, as a European, considers himself to be the representative of the superior/civilized race. The description, here, does not depict Africans as complete human beings rather they are depicted as physical fragments: "black limbs," "stamping feet," "rolling eyes". Conrad's description of the colonized is so biased that we never get to see an African man or woman in its completeness as if an entire and complete human identity is impossible in an African. Thus the image of Africa as civilized nation is missing in all the discourse about Africa. Chinua Achebe's novel *Things Fall Apart* (1958), in contrast to Conrad's description, presents Africans in a more positive light. *Things Fall Apart* was the first attempt to break the stereotypical image of a sinister, barbaric, primitive and barbaric Africa. The novel written by an African tries to 'write back' and subvert the colonial description of Africa by portraying it as civilized, developed and enlightened. Achebe, here, presents a wholly coherent African worldview in contrast to Conrad's *Heart of Darkness*. Achebe, here, artistically presents various customs and rituals that are a part of the civilized African society. The insider's view in *Things Fall Apart* helps us to break free from the bias and prejudice of the colonial discourse about Africa. His novel, as a representative postcolonial text, helps us look on the Africans from an African perspective without any prejudice or bias. And the "enthusiastic frenzy in a madhouse" of Conrad's *Heart of Darkness*, through postcolonial perspective of the Africans by Achebe, becomes a religious and civilized activity and it is the

European world that starts becoming bizarre. The attempt of the colonizers to control the religious and cultural life of the colonized gets ample manifestation in *Things Fall Apart*. Okonko's son Nwoye joins the Christian missionaries lead by Reverend James Smith. The conflict of the Africans with the Christian missionaries leads to the arrest and humiliation of the Umuofia leaders. Okonko, the protagonist, finally kills the court messenger to protect the dignity of his people.

CONCLUSION

To wrap up the discussion many things need to be brought together: the self-assumed superiority of the colonizers and their 'principle lie' for colonizing the weaker nation as a means of civilizing the barbarized, sinister, undeveloped and uncivilized people; and the efforts on the part of the downtrodden colonized to debunk this unjust representation of the colonized and their efforts to reinterpret and redefine their identity. It is an established fact that colonization was not wholly a civilizing mission but that it was actually an economic and exploitative enterprise. The colonizers instead of civilizing and enlightening the colonized exploited them economically, socially and politically. The colonizers colonized the natives at the level of the ideas: they tried to project that the Orient were barbarized, uncivilized, sinister and primitive, and that it was the "White Man's burden" to civilize them. The real motto behind the colonization was to exploit the resources, the riches and all other potentials of the weaker nations. Adam Smith and David Ricardo, right in the 18th century when the colonization was at its pinnacle, wrote books on the subject of economic exploitation of the weaker nations by the more powerful and supposedly- superior, civilized and enlightened nations. Their thesis was that imperialism/colonialism was not so much rooted in politics as in economics. Colonization was a phenomenon to exploit the resources of the weaker nations – selling their resources, raw material and using this raw material for running their own industries. The study of the colonial rule itself turns the argument of the colonizers on its head because it highlights how the mineral resources, raw materials were drained out by the colonizers to feed their own industries in England. Therefore, the colonies were exploited as resource labour power. Thus subaltern, the poorest of the poor, were greatly exploited. In all forms of literatures written after 1950s, we have the emphasis, expose of the colonialism. Writers like Raja Rao, Mulk Raj Anand, Chinua Achebe depict and highlight how the life of the poor colonized was conditioned, constrained, repressed, regressed by the dominant European colonial powers. They also debunked the distorted and biased representation of the Orient as savage, barbaric, primitive and uncivilized. They analyzed the works of the colonizers contrapuntally and thereby questioning the basic assumption of the colonial discourse that does not present the colonized in a positive light. However, we need to acknowledge the fact that though colonialism was largely an economic enterprise we cannot dismiss it as an exploitative enterprise altogether: there were many social evils that were prevalent in most of the colonies which needed to be redressed. The degeneration of the colonies is manifested through practices like Sati, slavery, and the like. The colonizers, in a way, played a deterministic role in abolishing such practices. But this should not mean that their rule over the weaker nations was a civilizing mission. According to Aime Cesaire, colonization far from civilizing the colonized decivilized the colonizer himself by degrading him, and by awakening his brutal instincts and moral relativism. Cesaire in *Discourse on Colonialism* states: "The fact is that the so-called European civilization…is incapable of solving the two major problems to which its existence has given rise: the problem of proletariat and the colonial problem; the Europe is unable to justify itself either before the bar of "reason" or before the bar of "conscience"; and that, increasingly, it takes refuge in a hypocrisy which is all the more odious because it is less and less likely to deceive…And today the indictment brought against it is not by the European masses alone, but on a world scale, by tens and tens of millions of men who, from the depths of slavery, set themselves up as judges." Thus by studying the reality/repercussions of colonialism on the colonized, it can be concluded that the stereotypical representation of the colonial rule as an enterprise to push back the frontiers of ignorance, disease, and tyranny in nothing but a lie. And neither is it "a philanthropic enterprise," nor "evangelization". I would end the chapter with a quotation from Aime Cesaire, whereby he artistically and subtly subverts/debunks the principle lie of the colonizer – the lie that the purpose of colonization was to civilize the barbaric, sinister, undeveloped, immature and uncivilized masses. Cesaire states: "And I say that between colonization and civilization there is an infinite distance; that out of all the colonial expedition that have been undertaken, out of all the colonial statutes that have been drawn up, out of all the memoranda that have been dispatched by all the ministers, there could not come a single human values."

References and Further Readings

Kipling, Rudyard. The Ballad of East and West. 1889.

Cesaire, Aime. Discourse on Colonialism. 1950.

Conrad, Joseph. Heart of Darkness. 1899.

Achebe, Chinua. Things Fall Apart. 1958.

Marx, Karl. The British Rule in India. 1853.

Gandhi, Mohandas K. Hind Swaraj or Indian Home Rule. 1909.

Raja, Rao. Kanthapura. 1938.

Achebe, Chinua. "An Image of Africa: Racism in Conrad's *Heart of Darkness*" in *Hopes and Impediments*. 1988.

Forster, E. M. A Passage to India. 1924.

Ashcroft, B; Griffiths, G; Tiffin, Helen. The Post-colonial Studies Reader. London: Routledge, 1995.

Derozio, Henry Louis Vivian. The Harp of India.

Tagore, Rabindranath. "Jana Gana Mana."

Macaulay, Thomas Babington. "Minutes Upon Indian Education". 1835.

CHAPTER III

Partition of India: A Tale of Mass Trauma, Exodus and Women's Exploitation.

Introduction

Many history books, novels, short stories, plays, poems and scholarly articles and papers etc have been written on the subject of Partition of India. Communal violence and bigotry has been one of the major themes of almost all these works. The entire process of Partition of India is not only a story of demographic change but also of the mass trauma, bigotry and violence that the people experienced during the course of Partition. I too shall try to give an insight into the horrors of Partition that resulted in mass trauma and exodus. The process of migration in the course of Partition was neither only about numbers nor was it only a quantitative movement. It was about how people suffered during the Partition riots as human beings. Most of the people migrated from one part of the country to the other in order to save themselves from the communal violence/riots that broke out in the course of the partition. Most of the people had to leave their homeland to settle in an alien country. This chapter, as the title suggests, is about the partition of India and how people suffered in the course of the partition. However, my focus in this chapter would be on the oppression and exploitation of the downtrodden women during the partition. In this chapter I would try to explore and highlight the hardships experienced by women during the partition of India and its aftermath. And how people specifically women suffered during their migration, how they were abducted by the members of the rival community and how they were raped, violated and their bodies dismembered and mutilated. The focus would also be on the violation of women not only by men of the rival communities but also by their own community members; and how their own family members were not willing to recover and reclaim them after their abduction because they thought that this would bring dishonor to their family. Thus I would focus on the aspect of Partition whereby women's body became a battle field for the members belonging to different communities.

Background

The plan for Partition of India began with the Mountbatten Plan in June 1947. In accordance with the plan, India was not going to remain united instead; it was to become divided into two parts – India and Pakistan. Pakistan was to be made up of two parts in the North West and the North East separated by 1000 miles. Punjab and Bengal with their small Muslim majorities were to be divided and Muslim majority parts given to Pakistan. To devise all this and to facilitate such a major change, a boundary commission was set up. This boundary commission was specifically set up to draw the borders in Punjab and Bengal. Cyril Radcliffe, a British civil servant, was made the chairman of the commission. It was Cyril Fielding who was given the final say after getting advice from both the Hindu and the Muslim members of the Commission. This boundary Commission had many problems to begin with. First of all, Radcliffe had never been to India and therefore he was completely ignorant of the ground reality. He was a complete outsider and did not know anything substantial about India. Since he did not know the ground reality, he was not able to take many decisions judiciously. Another problem of the Radcliffe Commission was that Radcliffe had to work with outdated maps and census figures. Moreover he had to produce a report within a short span of time. The most crucial factor was that he was an English man and he was completely biased towards propagating and promoting the interests of the British. As a result, neither the interests of Pakistan nor of India were, in a way, taken into account as he was devising boundaries and he was going to redraw map of the Indian Subcontinent.

Certain Decisions Undertaken by the Radcliffe Commission

Most of the decisions taken by the Radcliffe Commission were devastating. Radcliffe was dictated by Mountbatten to specifically use religious demography as the main criteria in boundary making. The criteria, was definitely not going to be political, social, cultural and linguistic instead it was going to be religious. Almost 62% of Punjab was allotted to India whereas the rest was given to Pakistan. Moreover, the division of various infrastructure related projects, irrigation system, infrastructure of Punjab and Bengal – all this was divided irrespective of the fact that it was not going to be functional anymore in divided format. The new boundaries that were drawn passed through not only farms and villages but also through houses/homes thereby, eradicating the very notion and concept of human and just Partition. Millions of Hindus and Muslims were left on the wrong side of the border which was a very painful/awful experience for those people. While Pakistan got the Provinces of Sind, Baluchistan, North-Western Frontier, West Punjab and East Bengal; Eastern Pakistan was separated by the rest of Pakistan by 1000 miles of Indian territory which was an impractical way of drawing boundaries. Shauna Singh Baldwin rightly and aptly highlights and criticizes the impractical and inhumane Partition of India into three parts:

"Seventy-three days to cut a land in three, East Pakistan, India and West Pakistan, like cutting arms from a man."

Creation of Refugees

This entire process resulted in 5 million Muslims in India and 5 million Hindus in Pakistan migrating to the alternate country and in this entire process, Sikhs were largely ignored. Moreover, the entire process of Partition resulted in a very pathetic event and process – the creation of the 'refugee'. Becoming a refugee became a sad reality for a vast amount/number of population. Partition by creating borders and later restrictions on mobility, created two categories of 'citizens' and 'non-citizens' as well as 'stateless people' whom neither India nor Pakistan identified with. And this mass of people came to be termed by the Government of India as 'displaced persons,' 'migrants,' and 'refugees'. These 'displaced' and 'stateless people' suffered a lot in the course of Partition.

Aftermath of Partition: Mass violence and Exodus.

After the Partition of India in August 1947, incidents of mass violence and bigotry spread all over India especially in the northern and eastern India with mass, migration/exodus taking place. Punjab specifically became a site of some worst violence incidents and calamity. The first incidents of violence however, can actually be traced to pre Partition Bengal where serious rioting took place as early as 1946 in the course of Provincial elections and hence initiated a process which ultimately culminated in the Partition riots, mass trauma and exodus in 1947 on the ground that had already been prepared in 1946 and, which had deliberately been left unchecked by the colonial regime. The entire process radically and drastically changed the demography of the Indian Sub-continent. There were many places from where people fled in order to save their honour and lives. Many places like Delhi soon became a place where one could hardly find any craftsmen like carpenters, masons, tailors, etc as most of them were Muslims and they had migrated to Pakistan in the course of Partition riots.

Based on the 1951 census of displaced persons, 7,226,000 Muslims had gone to Pakistan from India and more than 7,249,000 Hindus and Sikhs had fled to India from Pakistan. This traumatic exodus took pace immediately after the partition of India as people somehow wanted to migrate to the areas/states that they found would be better for them and for the generations to come. Thus one can easily imagine the sad/pathetic reality that was taking place on both sides of the border. Around 11.2 million or 78% of population transfer took place in the Punjab province/region alone. Whereas 5.3 million Muslims moved from India to West Punjab in Pakistan, almost 3.4 million Hindus and Sikhs moved from Pakistan to East Punjab now in India. The images of long foot caravans, overloaded carts and trucks and, overflowing trains immediately comes to one's mind when one visualizes the 'journey'.

Unity between Different Communities Came to an End

The entire process of Partition of India is not only a story of demographic change but also of the mass trauma, bigotry and violence that the people experienced during the course of Partition. The Partition had been done on communal lines. During the split of India, there was a mass migration of over 15 million. Since the partition was done on communal lines and boundaries had been drawn in accordance with that plan/pattern, the Muslims obviously were leaving India to settle in Pakistan and likewise the Hindus were leaving for India. Therefore, the entire process of exodus was not happening silently, smoothly and peacefully. The entire process of Partition – the creation of Pakistan – was tumultuous which resulted in large scale violence, chaos, riots, deaths and heinous crimes against humanity. This, in turn, deepened the rift between the Hindus and the Muslims and thereby shacking and destroying the unity that had been a result of more than hundred years of joint struggle against the colonial regime. The process of communalism had started much earlier than 1940s and in fact it had started by the end of the 19th century itself when the sense of communal identity was hardening and deepening among people belonging to different communities.

The 'Journey'

The communal gap was, in a way, further widened by the colonial philosophy of 'divide and rule'. The mob of people that had to leave their native places was threatened by the rival communities who could attack them not only in their native places but also on their way to their destined nation/province. The entire journey was not only characterized by feeling of loss of homeland but also there was a traumatic feeling of uncertainty and threat as what would happen to them on the way especially when women and children were accompanying them. The entire journey was marked with violence and bigotry and Partition process certainly left both the countries – India and Pakistan – devastated socially, politically and economically. Many inhuman atrocities were committed by one community on the people belonging to other communities. Many women were mercilessly and repeatedly raped and then ruthlessly butchered. Bapsi Sidhwa in her novel *Ice-Candy-Man* artistically and subtly presents such incidents of violence specifically the violence against women. The train episode presented in the novel is one such episode where we find the violation of women: "A train from Gurdaspur has just come…Everyone in it is dead…butchered…two gunny bags full of women's breasts." This mass trauma not only did add to the chaos but also made the life of most of the people so miserable that it is, in a way, not possible to express such traumatic feelings and experiences in words. The communal riots were characterized by the bombing of immigrants, and filling trains full of dismembered bodies and then sending them across the border. This had become a regular feature and both the countries witnessed a no of such incidents in the course of the Partition. This finds ample description in Bapsi Sidhwa's *Ice-Candy-Man* when the protagonist of the novel states: "I'll tell you to your face – I lose my senses when I think of the mutilated bodies on that train from Gurdaspur…that might I went mad, I tell you, I lobbed grenades through the windows of Hindu and Sikh I'd known all my life! I hated their guts."

Communal Violence and Bigotry

In the entire course of violence that happened during and immediately after the Partition of India, more than one million people were killed in Punjab alone. Almost 12 million people were left homeless and thousands were raped. Revenge killings became a very common phenomenon and they took place in different parts of the country. Moreover, various sporadic incidents took place in other parts of northern India as news of the violence spread rapidly across the country and there began a 'chain reaction action'. This chain reaction was particularly strong in those states that were experiencing Partition especially in the northern and the eastern parts of the country. Bapsi Sidhwa artistically portrays the intercommunity violence that had become commonplace during the course of the partition of India in her novel *Ice-Candy-Man*. The episode in which the Sikhs attack the Muslim village Pir Pindo and when Ranna a small boy, wounded runs for life presents perhaps the vilest side of communal discord. She writes:

"There were too many ugly and abandoned children like him scavenging in the looted houses and the rubble of burnt-out buildings. His rages clinging to his wounds, straw sticking in the scalped skull, Ranna wondered through the lanes stealing chapattis and grain from houses strewn with dead bodies rifling the corpses for anything he could use... No one minded the semi-naked specter as he looked in doors with his knowing, wide-set peasant eyes."

Gendered Realities of 'Honour' Killings and Violence.

During the course of the communal bigotry, violence and riots, there were many families and communities which were taking decision to kill members of their own family and these members were invariably women and children as it was thought that they would fall prey to the frenzied mob of the rival community. Therefore they thought that it was better for them to get killed by their own family members rather than expose them to rape and murder by the male members of the rival community who were bent upon destroying the chastity of the women of the other communities by polluting and violating them. The people feared that their women and children would be abducted, probably converted, raped and impregnated by the men of other religion. Therefore, in order to avoid such circumstances and acts of heinous crime, the harsh decision was immediately and repeatedly taken by a number of families belonging to different communities. Many writers have portrayed such incidents in their works and in this connection, Bapsi Sidhwa's novel *Ice-Candy-Man* proves to be a realistic documentation of the heinous crime committed on women. In this novel Pir Pindo, a Muslim village, is attacked by the Sikhs. The Muslims of the village are killed, their women gang-raped. Men, women and children are ruthlessly and mercilessly butchered. Women are so badly treated and harassed that it is decided that the women and girls of Pir Pindo would gather at Choudhary's house and pour kerosene oil around the house to burn themselves.

Reasons and instances of Self-Inflicting Violence and 'Honour' Killings of Women.

During the process and course of Partition, killings of women in fact, became one of the ways of saving the honour of the women, the religion and the country of different communities before they decided to migrate to India or Pakistan. A large numbers of instances of self-inflicting violence can be seen in many documentations of violence during the course of Partition. For instance, Mangal Singh from a village near the Gurdaspur border along his two brothers killed as many as eighteen members of their family by gathering them together in a gurduwara and praying for their souls, and finally putting them to death. There are many other such incidents that have been recorded and there is a possibility that many such incidents may have occurred during the course of Partition that has not been recorded, when in the vitiated atmosphere insanity prevailed and men lost their sanity. In her famous work *What the Body Remembers*, Shauna Singh Baldwin artistically and subtly shows how the male members of the society/community killed their own women ruthlessly: Papaji kills his daughter-in-law Kusum in order to avoid her body being violated by men of the other community:

"Papaji thinks that for good-good women, death should be
preferable to dishonor."

Such incidents were projected as examples of women's
heroism and courage. Such incidents highlight the violence that was
wrecked against women during the partition of India. The fact is that
this violence against women was not only being inflicted by the
members of the rival communities but by the members of their own
communities who did not want, at any cost, their women and
children to fall prey to the lust of the rival community members and
suffer rest of their lives. Therefore, out of the fear of such incidents,
they thought it better to kill them with their own hands. Many
historians and writers have now started talking about this new kind
of violence, where women and children were mercilessly killed by
the members of their own communities and most often by their own
family members. This aspect of Partition must not be overlooked
and the need of the hour is to take deeper interest and do deeper
research into such incidents of violence that was inflicted by the
male members of these families. These incidents are not seen as
violence but as 'hounour' killings and the death of the women is
usually projected as martyrdom and as the best service that they
could have done to their families, community and to the motherland.
A scholar who has worked extensively in this field is Urvashi
Butalia. She has spoken at length as to how the violence of
communities towards their own people and specifically towards
women became a norm during the Partition of India. According to
Urvashi Butalia, there is an immense need to address the violence of
the communities towards their own people particularly, women and
children who were considered as weak and vulnerable. She refutes
the projection that the women came out in defense of nationalism,
the community and the religion by sacrificing their own lives. While

many women must have died unwillingly without even knowing that this was the fatal fate which was waiting for them There is an immense need to address the violence of the communities towards their own people particularly women and children, it was projected as if they were doing this all in the name of respect towards their families, their elders and towards the society at large as well as to save the honour of their religion and community. Another sad story of ninety women of the little village of Thoa Khalsa, which was near Rawalpindi, who drowned themselves by jumping into a well during the communal riots to save themselves from being violated and raped by the members of the rival communities in the course of Partition. This has aptly been depicted in the novel *Tamas* by Bhisham Sahni. However, such representations as has been pointed out by Urvashi Bhutalia, do not project the complete picture and in fact, they hide the reality that must have existed on the ground. An important question that arises here is that whether women took the extreme step of jumping into the well voluntarily or it was out of social pressure? Was it that they, out of the fear of being violated, wanted to end their lives or that they were being forced to do that? This is the question that largely remains unanswered. Moreover, histories of such heroism are repeatedly woven to hide the horror of such violence. One may talk about mob violence, Partition violence, killings, rapes, pillaging that was conducted by the members of one community over the members of the other community, but one must not completely ignore the violence committed on women and children by their own community. It was extremely horrible that women were being killed by their own family members and deeper analysis and research needs to be done into such incidents of self-inflicting violence and 'honour' killings.

Intra-community Violence

A very important aspect that has emerged over the years is that after the partition of India numerous incidents of intra-community violence have occurred. Intra-community violence simply refers to the violence inflicted on people not by the members of their rival communities but by their own community members who were supposed to protect and shield them from the violence of other communities. Some very interesting stories have been written on this aspect of Partition violence. Sadat Hassan Manto, the well known writer who migrated to Pakistan after the partition, has artistically and aptly portrayed this aspect of violence in his stories. For instance, the story entitled "*Khol Do*" tells the story of a young girl Sakina daughter of Sirajuddin, who is repeatedly raped not by the members of the rival communities but by the men of her own community who were supposed to protect her. While the community was supposed to protect her from the Partition violence and take her to safer horizon, she falls prey to the men from her own community. Manto, therefore, highlights and condemns the hollowness and sterility of the patriarchal society in which women were safe neither in their own community nor among their rival communities. By presenting such incidents in their works the writers try to bring to light the fact that women were not victimized by the men of the rival communities alone, but they were not safe in their own communities and that they have been greatly wronged especially during the tumultuous times of Partition. Another problem that women faced during the course of Partition and aftermath is that woman simply being married to a person who wished to settle or had attempted to settle in the other country, often lost the citizenship of the country in which they had been originally/already residing. Not only did they lose the citizenship of the country but also were separated from their family, friends, neighbours and their loved ones. This feeling of loss of homeland and the loss of the loved ones still haunts the people who somehow survived the Partition of India.

Mob Frenzy and Women's Bodies

As has already been pointed out, the process of migration/exodus of people from one country to the other country did not go smoothly and peacefully. Women in particular were vulnerable in the mass movement of people across the borders. They were often abducted and taken away from their family/community members by the attackers of the rival community. A very common feature and sad reality that occurred during the course of the partition characterized by chaos and confusion was the violation and rape of women. It became a common occurrence and it was, in a way, an indirect way for men of one community to attack the male members of the other community because by violating the downtrodden bodies of the women, men of the rival community thought that they had completed the project and that they had taken revenge from the rival community members. This again has artistically portrayed by many writers in their works. Alok Bhalla, for instance in his work *Partition Dialogues: Memories of a Lost Home* states:

"Victories are celebrated on the bodies of women... When women are attacked, it is not they *per se* who are targets but the men to whom they belong." (Bhalla, 233)

Bapsi Sidhwa also depicts a similar kind of incident in her novel *Ice-Candy-Man* when Ayah, the protagonist, is raped by the members of the rival community:

"They drag Ayah out. They drag her by her arms… her bare feet – that want to move backwards – are forced forward. Her lips are drawn away from her teeth, and the resisting curve of her throat opens her mouth like dead child's scream. Four men stand pressed against her… their lips stretched in triumphant grimances."

Various incidents of such violence have come to light with the efforts of many scholars who have conducted in depth study/research on the subject. There have occurred incidents of violence whereby women's breasts have been cut off, their bodies being tattooed with the marks and symbols of the rival communities and other religion, their bodies being mutilated and dismembered as if a battle was being fought between men on the bodies of women. Moreover the men had become so callous that they would display the dismembered bodies of women at public places. They were free to do anything, and they were free to violate and cut the bodies of the women of the rival communities. Such incidents of brutality and heinous crime resulted in the 'honour' killings of women by their own family members. The women were killed in order to save them from such incidents of rape and tattooing because their male family members thought that it was better to kill women rather than make them exposed to the uncivilized and frenzied rival community male members.

Women's Bodies and the Battle between Men

Rape, as has been pointed out, had become common place. Most of the women experienced it and lived with its consequences individually for a very long time to come. As a result the psyche of women continues to experience the pain, caused by the insane brutalities that had been committed on them during the Partition, which was difficult to explain in words. All those women who had experienced such scenes and even if they had not experienced it themselves but have seen or heard of such incidents happening to others, kept on suffering in silence and it took them decades or maybe they never were able to come out of the trauma easily. So, the battles that were being fought over female bodies continued unabated and the personal narratives of women who have experienced the partition violence brings to light the ways in which female bodies are equated with notions of home, religious communities, nations and national territories. Whereas the trend had emerged in the 19th century whereby women became the hallmark of nation, women became the symbol of nationality, the same ideology continued in the 20th century. Now, in the course of violence also, it was women's bodies that had to bear the brunt of the entire process painfully. Urvashi Bhutalia aptly states:

"Violence against women becomes a means of feminization of women's male counterparts who prove incapable of protecting 'their' women/community/nation." (Bhutalia, 1998)

So men of one community took extreme pride in disrespecting, raping and tattooing women of the other community because they thought that this would, in turn, prove the point that men of those communities were so weak, they were so chicken-hearted and, they were so feminized that they were unable to save the honour of their women. This, in turn, was going to be a great celebration for the men of that community which was inflicting all these sufferings on the downtrodden and oppressed women. Urvashi Bhutalia goes on to say:

"Most studies of the Partition violence in India documents the instances of killing and looting but do not categorize acts such as mass drowning among women as violent acts which are projected as bravery undertaken to protect one's honour which in the case of women is inextricably tied to their community." (Bhutalia: 1993)

Therefore another sad reality of communalism was that most of the attackers were not outsiders rather they were known people, they were fellow villagers, neighbours and friends who used the lawlessness of the times as an opportunity to grab property as well as to force women into marriages and to assault their sexuality.

Abduction of Women during Partition and the Indifference of Their Own Family Members

The reality of attacks and abduction of women has a different story to tell. Some of the families, whose women were forcibly abducted, initially reported their disappearance. But there were some families who avoided that because they thought that this would bring dishonour to their family. Therefore, the loss/ disappearance of women from their family was hardly of any significance if the issue of honour was at stake. This conflict between honour and saving the life of women became a great problem because for those women who were abducted, mostly there was no one to recover and reclaim them, no one to revolt about their missing. On the contrary, if it was a male member who had been abducted, then the report was lodged immediately and their family members would leave no stone unturned in order to recover and reclaim him. However, there was no such hunt for the missing women. The reason behind all this indifference and callousness was that it was thought that the missing women must have been dirtied and violated by the rival community male members. As a result, there was no place for such women in their family anymore. Even in cases where some reporting was done, and if the women were found, if they were in a bad shape, dishevelled, the family would decide not to take them back because they thought that it was better to avoid such polluted females back in the family as they must have lived with or been raped and violated by the men of the other community. Therefore, the entire notion of humanity was relegated into the background when it came to the issue of reclaiming lost women. This indifferent attitude of society towards the downtrodden women has artistically been portrayed in Jyotirmoyee Devi's *The River Churning: A Partition Novel* (1967): Sutara, who has been violated by the members of the rival community suffers social rejection by her own community.

Restoration of Abducted Women

The term 'abducted person' referred to a male child and, a woman of any age who had been separated from his or her family and made to reside forcibly with a person or a family from the other community after the date of March 1, 1947. During the course of communal riots that broke out during the partition of India, as has already been pointed out, numerous incidents of abduction of women and children and their forcible conversion to the other religion came to light. The restoration of these abducted persons was one of the major problems that the governments of the newly formed nations faced. The major problem was that once a person was declared abducted, it became the responsibility of the state to recover and restore such person. In this connection, Urvashi Bhutalia states:

"Elaborate arrangements were made to get 'our women' back, irrespective of their own decision to remain where they were, and also irrespective of the fact that their families might not accept these 'fallen women' back."

Need to Study the Hardships of the Migrants Who Survived the Partition Violence

A lot has been stated about violence about the migration/exodus, mob frenzy and incidents of rape that took place in the course of the partition of India but as has been pointed out by Gargi Chakravarthy too much focus has been laid on physical abuse of women which is valid and relevant but equally important to discuss are the ways in which the uprooted women have faced the enormous challenge of rebuilding and reshaping their lives in alien conditions and how some of their concerns shaped a new women's movement . Gargi Chakravarthy points out how in the entire course of discussion and historiography that has appeared on the theme of Partition, there has been so much focus on violence and on various hardships that people underwent but not upon how these migrants survived and what they went through in their new found country. So how these migrants survived in Pakistan or in India is a subject that needs to be looked into with greater detail. However, the study of their survival itself would reveal the hardships that they experienced during their journey towards their destined country.

Conclusion

To conclude it can be said that Partition resulted in a large scale violence and exodus. The process of mass migration did not run peacefully which resulted in mass trauma whereby women were abducted, raped, tattooed and then mercilessly butchered. The men and children were killed. Revenge killings became common place. The houses and markets were set ablaze. Most of the people suffered in one way or the other in the course of the Partition. Women in particular were victimized both by their rival communities and by the members of their own community. Men belonging to the rival communities violated them in order to send a message to other communities that they have not been able to protect their women and their own community. This phenomenon/process of violation of women during Partition of India became commonplace and it was, in a way, an indirect way for men of one community to attack the male members of the other community because by violating the downtrodden bodies of the women, men of the rival community thought that they had completed the project and that they had taken revenge from the rival community members. Their miseries and exploitation did not end here. As the violation of women by the male members of other religion became common place, it resulted in the process whereby their own family members killed them in order to save them from possible rape, tattooing and murder. There were families who killed their own women claiming that they were protecting them from possible rape, impregnation, pollution and violation and thereby they silenced the histories of these women forever. These women continued to exist only in memories but in reality they refused to exist, they were not allowed to exist and there was no one to remember them. It can be said that the class of people who suffered the most during the communal Partition riots/violence is that of women. Thus, there is an immense need to understand the entire process from the aspect of gendered violence inflicted both by the rival communities as well as by their own community. I would conclude the chapter with a Quotation from Mushirul Hasan:

"The history books do not record the pain, trauma and sufferings of those who had to part from their kin, friends and neighbours, their deepening nostalgia for places they had lived in for generations, the anguish of devotees removed from their places of worship, and the harrowing experiences of the countless people who boarded trains thinking they would be transported to the realizations of their dreams, but of whom not a man, woman or child survived the journey."

References and Further Readings

Baldwin, Shauna Singh. *What the Body Remembers*. New Delhi, Harper Collins. 1999.

Bhalla, Alok, ed. *Partition Dailogues: Memories of a Lost Home*. New Delhi: Oxford UP, 2006.

Sidhwa, Bapsi. *Ice-Candy-Man*. New Delhi, Penguin Books. 1989.

Hasan, Mushirul. *India's Partition: Process, Strategy and Mobilization*. Oxford University Press. 1993.

Bhutalia, Urvashi. *The Other Side of Silence: Voices from the Partition of India*.

Devi, Jyotirmoyee. *The River Churning: A Partition Novel*. Trans. Enakshi Chaterjee. New Delhi. 1995.

Menon, Ritu; Bhasin, Kamala. *Borders and Boundaries: Women in India's Partition*. New Delhi. 1998.

Chakravarthy, Gargi. *Coming Out of Partition – Refugee Women*. Srishti Publishers and Distributors. 2005.

Sahni, Bhisham. *Tamas* (Darkness).

Manto, Sadat Hasan. *Khol Do*.

Select Bibliography and Further Readings

The Author takes great pleasure in acknowledging his indebtedness to the following sources the preparation of this book:

Friedan, Betty. *The Feminine Mystique*. W. W. Norton and Co. 1963.

Wollstonecraft, Mary. *A Vindication of the Rights of Women*. 1792.

Gregory, John. *A Father's Legacy To His Daughters*.

Rousseau, Jean-Jaques. *Emile, Or On Education*. 1762.

Woolf, Virginia. *A Room of One's Own*. 1929.

Ibsen, Henric. A Doll's House. 1879.

Narayan, R. K. The Painter of Signs.1976.

Adichie, Chimamanda Ngogi. *We Should All Be Feminist*.2014.

Beauvoir, Simone de. *The Second Sex*. Translated by Constance Borde and Sheila Malovancy-Chevallier; with an introduction by Judith Thurman.

Barre, Francois, Poullain de la. The Equality of the Two Sexes.1673

Anthony, Susan B; Stanton, Elizabeth Candy. *The Revolution*. 1868-72.

Balzac, Honore de. *Letters of Two Brides*; translated by R. S. Scott.

Child, Lydia, Maria. The History of the Condition of Women, in Various Ages and Nations

Kipling, Rudyard. The Ballad of East and West. 1889.

Cesaire, Aime. Discourse on Colonialism. 1950.

Conrad, Joseph. Heart of Darkness. 1899.

Achebe, Chinua. Things Fall Apart. 1958.

Marx, Karl. The British Rule in India. 1853.

Gandhi, Mohandas K. Hind Swaraj or Indian Home Rule. 1909.

Raja, Rao. Kanthapura. 1938.

Achebe, Chinua. "An Image of Africa: Racism in Conrad's *Heart of Darkness*" in *Hopes and Impediments*. 1988.

Forster, E. M. A Passage to India. 1924.

Ashcroft, B; Griffiths, G; Tiffin, Helen. The Post-colonial Studies Reader. London: Routledge, 1995.

Derozio, Henry Louis Vivian. The Harp of India.

Tagore, Rabindranath. "Jana Gana Mana."

Macaulay, Thomas Babington. "Minutes Upon Indian Education". 1835.

Baldwin, Shauna Singh. *What the Body Remembers*. New Delhi, Harper Collins. 1999.

Bhalla, Alok, ed. *Partition Dailogues: Memories of a Lost Home.* New Delhi: Oxford UP, 2006.

Sidhwa, Bapsi. *Ice-Candy-Man.* New Delhi, Penguin Books. 1989.

Hasan, Mushirul. *India's Partition: Process, Strategy and Mobilization.* Oxford University Press. 1993.

Bhutalia, Urvashi. *The Other Side of Silence: Voices from the Partition of India.*

Devi, Jyotirmoyee. *The River Churning: A Partition Novel.* Trans. Enakshi Chaterjee. New Delhi. 1995.

Menon, Ritu; Bhasin, Kamala. *Borders and Boundaries: Women in India's Partition.* New Delhi. 1998.

Chakravarthy, Gargi. *Coming Out of Partition – Refugee Women.* Srishti Publishers and Distributors. 2005.

Sahni, Bhisham. *Tamas* (Darkness).

Manto, Sadat Hasan. *Khol Do.*